OCEAN
of
Possibilities

Wyatt & Sons Publishers books may be ordered through booksellers or by contacting:

Wyatt & Sons Publishers, LLC
Mobile, Alabama 36695
www.wyattpublishing.com
editor@wyattpublishing.com

Because of the dynamic nature of the Internet, any web address or links contained in this book may have changed since publication and may no longer be valid.

Cover illustrations by: Nancy Neres
Cover design by: Mark Wyatt
Interior design by: Mark Wyatt
ISBN 13:978-1-954798-23-6

Printed in the United States of America

INSTITUTE FOR DISABILITY STUDIES
THE UNIVERSITY OF SOUTHERN MISSISSIPPI

OCEAN
of Possibilities

**Written and Illustrated by
the Hurricane Buddies of
West Harrison High School**

WS
**WYATT & SONS
PUBLISHERS, LLC**
Mobile, Alabama
www.wyattpublishing.com

Dream Job

by Brionna McLaurin

I love to help little kids and help them open their stuff and help them get out their mats. I put the cover on them and then when they wake up I will help them put up their mat. I help them open their snacks. I take them outside and wait for the bell when their parents come.

Future Dream Businesses

by Brionna McLaurin

Hairstylist,
Making dreads,
Practice on my brother's hair,
"Brionna's Hair Salon"

Real estate agent,
Selling houses,
Start business at 21 years old.

Future Dream Business

by Brionna McLaurin

Feeding the Turtles

by Brionna McLaurin

We fed the turtles
I felt happy
They were eating the food
Reminded me of sea turtles

I saw a bird and 3 turtles
Someone playing football
When we walked to go to the turtles
Rate today a 10

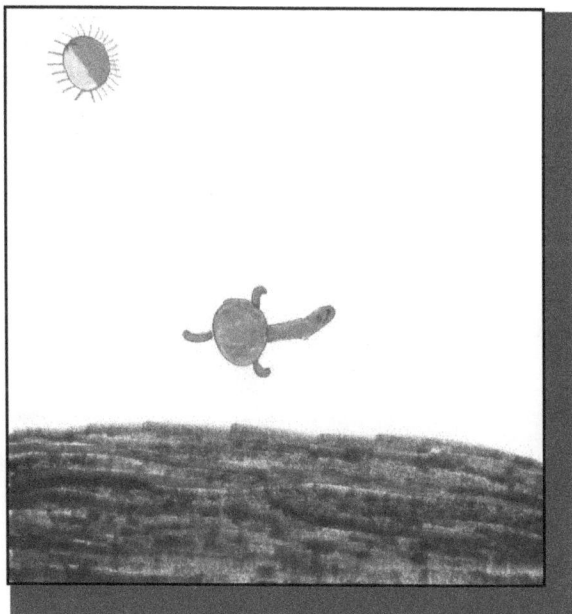

T-Topia and Dreams

by Jackson Dye

I enjoyed working at T-Topia.

I showed people what size clothes they need.

I like helping people.

My dream job is working at Chick- fil-A.

Most fun: bringing people their orders and making the food

Most challenging: cleaning the place

Inspiration: my brother. He used to work there, and he's already in the fire academy.

Idea: I was thinking if I can work his old job

The Turtle's Journey

by Jackson Dye

I woke up one morning and I am a little turtle
swimming in a pond.
Me and all my turtle friends were swimming together
Taking a journey across the great coral reef,
Exploring the great ocean sea.
We met a lot of other sea animals in the coral reef,
Swimming along and seeing a lot of plants, animals,
And a lot of other things in the ocean.
We were having a great time in the coral reef.

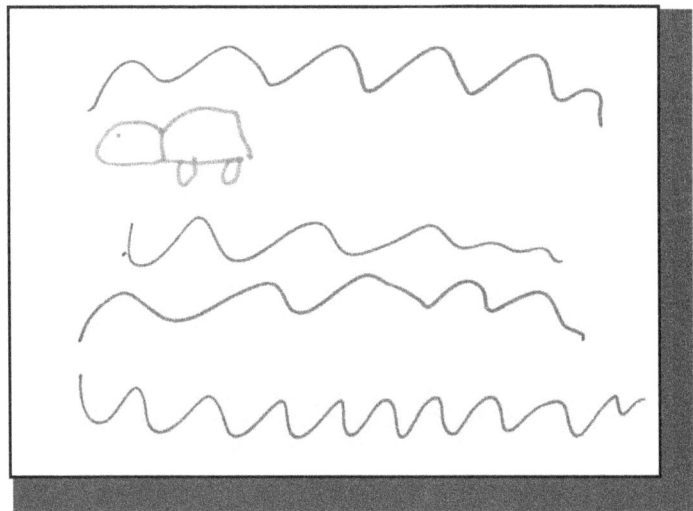

I Met A Robot

by Jada Lawrence

I met a robot

She was nice

Our first adventure was going to the zoo

And our second adventure was going to the water park

But me and my robot friend became best friends.

Underwater Career

by Jada Lawrence

A Day in the Life of an Underwater Photographer

I will wear a diver's suit and it will be pink. I go underwater to take pictures of the animals. I will not go in the deep-sea part because I cannot see in the deep water, so I will just stay in the light part of the ocean. I will take pictures of fish, sea turtles, octopus, all the sea creatures, even dolphins, they're cute. I would see a magical fish unicorn and it would be pink with a purple horn and purple hair. The unicorn fish likes to swim in the ocean.

Talking Animals: A Zoo Adventure

by Jada Lawrence

I am stuck in a zoo and all the animals can talk.

The lions were talking about how to survive in the wild.

The monkeys were laughing at my jokes

and I was laughing at their jokes.

The hyenas were laughing at me

because I was stuck in the zoo with them.

The koalas were cute and sweet and had soft fur.

The sloth were old and mean and bad.

Feeding the Turtles

by Courtlan Belcher

Turtles.

Happy.

Lake.

Feed.

Cabbage.

Turtles.

Go again.

Happy.

Underwater Careers

by Courtlan Belcher

I am a space explorer in space.

I am going to have fun under the water with an octopus.

Artwork

Spiderman

by Dawson Peoples

Spiderman.

Uses his spider webs.

Good at fighting.

The job that Spiderman will be good at will be

Firefighter.

If I were Spiderman, I would help people in need.

I will try to put out the fire with spider webs.

I would climb buildings to find people who need help.

I would drive the fire truck.

Ninja Turtle Adventure

by Dawson Peoples

Ninja Turtle

Blue costume

Fight

Help all people

Teamwork

Friends

Eat pizza

Doors of Possibilities

by Dawson Peoples

Chef

Cook food and recipes

Baking

Go through the door

School then work

My Dream Job

by Donovan Jones

I will be a captain of a boat who has a hat and drives and also maintains order on the water. I will captain my boat. I would feel happy. I will have other marines working for me. It will be a great day. I will fish, I will take my boat out, I would do cargo travels. I would do boating, and bring my boat back to the dock.

Underwater Career

by Donovan Jones

I would go under the water, taking pictures of the animals:
Octopus, sea turtles, dolphins, fish.
Favorite color fish is orange.
Coral reef. Starfish. Dive.
Air tank to breathe.
Waterproof camera.
Shark.
Run away!

The Turtle's Dream

by Donavon Jones

My turtle's dream is that he wants to be a basketball
player. He did do it. He trained. He dribbled the ball
and he shoot the ball. His name was Joel. Joel was on a
basketball team. He just dribbles and shoots the ball.
Joel the Turtle felt really excited and surprised, smiling.
He became famous. His family was very excited he was
the famous basketball player turtle.

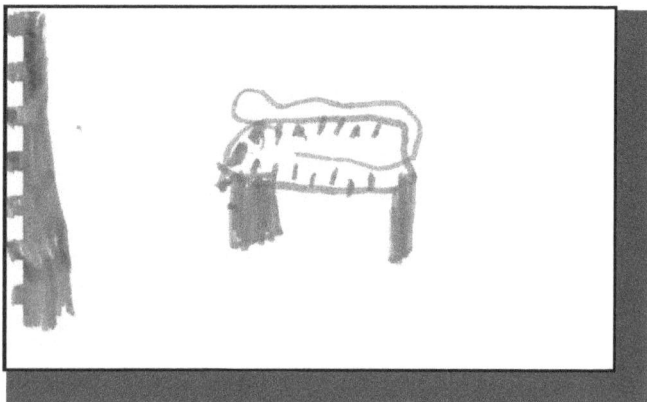

Joel the Turtle Basketball Player

Experience at WaySubs!

by FaBien McKenzie

I like serving and preparing the sandwiches.

I liked the customer experience too.

I see myself as an employee working as a server.

I would like to work mornings because during the night,

I am very sleepy.

I would like to work with a team because the job will

become easier.

I would not accept to work overtime or working nights.

What makes me nervous is the interview process.

I would like to find a job, obtain my driver's license, and

to pursue a Mechanical school.

The Turtle's Dream

by FaBien McKenzie

The turtle dreamed he could walk on land,

To see a lot of things they don't normally

Get to see in the water.

I like to explore nature like the turtle.

Birds—robins, pigeons, eagles—

I like the different sounds they make and their patterns.

I like watching turtles eat and being in nature;

It makes me feel excellent.

Happy Turtle

by FaBienMcKenzie

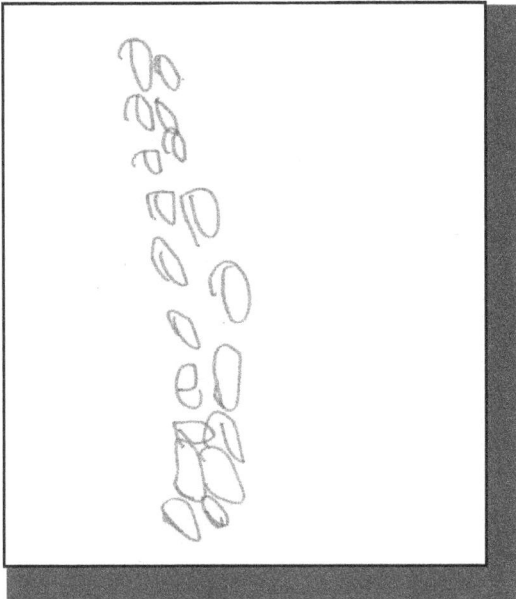

Brown Turtles on the Move
by Juan Serrano-Garcia

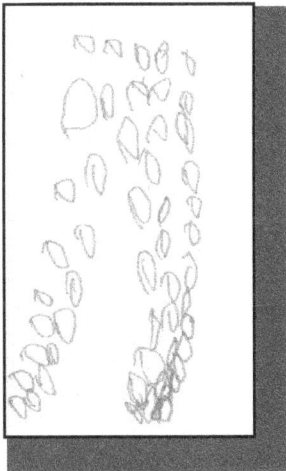

Green Turtles- Teamwork
by Juan Serrano-Garcia

My Dream Job

by Kennedi Flowers

A cook

Spaghetti

Hamburgers and steak.

Name of restaurant:

Goods and Fish

Drinks: Orange, grapes, and apples

Clothing to wear: shorts for customers

Sweatpants and a shirt for workers

Blue pants, purple shirts for workers

Ninja Turtle, Happy Life

by Kennedi Flowers

I'm a ninja turtle

I'll feed the turtles with seeds

Grass seeds

I feed a snake

I feed them seeds, carrots

I feed the rabbit carrots

I'll go play volleyball

On a team with my buddy, Kathy

I hit a ball. I hit it in their fence.

I won.

Happy life.

Dream Job at Raising Cane's

by Kennedi Flowers

Raising Cane's

Because I get to cook the

Chicken

Bread

And fries.

Make money.

Wash dishes

Sweep

Clean up.

by Kennedi Flowers

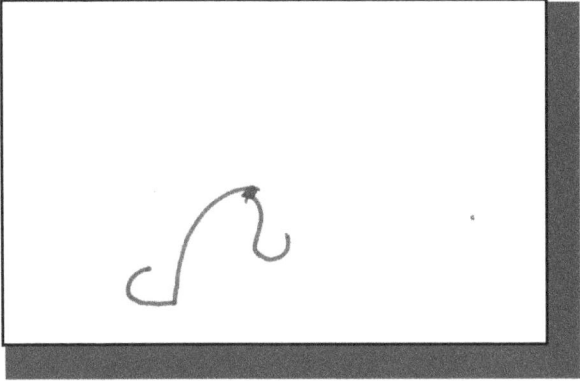

My Friend, the Turtle
by LaDevion Leggett

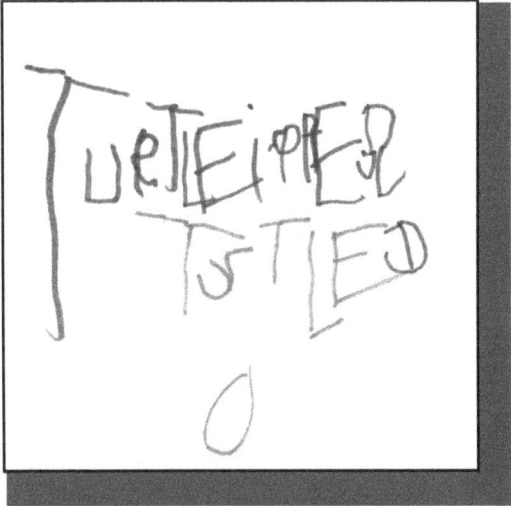

Turtle, Turtles, Turtles
by LaDevion Leggett

Turtle Trek

by Makayla Harris

As a turtle, I will live in a pond with my family.
I will have a lot of friends like alligators and fish.
I swim and slide in the brown water of the pond.
I like eating grass that is very big on the cool day with my cousins.

Makayla's Fishing School

by Makayla Harris

My favorite hobby is catching fish. I was two when I started. I will start a business teaching people how to catch fish.

First, we have to go to the lake. Next, we are going to learn how to use a fishing pole, learn how to hook the worm onto the fishing line, and then we are going to learn how to throw it out and reel it in. Then we will catch some fish and place the fish in a bucket. Then, we are going to show you how to skin the fish.

They'll need to wear boots because they're going to be in the mud. They don't have to be; they can be on the docks, but mostly, you're going to be in the water or in the boat.

Each fish will cost $60.

At the end of the day, I never get tired because I am just used to it.

I have been fishing since I was two.

by Makayla Harris

Two Dream Careers

by Makayla Harris

Work with animals.

Be a vet.

Do the checkups.

To make sure they are healthy.

Makayla' s Clinic

Clinic will be painted white and pink.

A lot of pictures of animals on the wall.

Horses, dogs, cats

Or work at a Daycare

I like hanging out with kids

If they cry, I will play with toys with them

or tell them to lay down and take a nap.

My Job As A Space Explorer

by Malachi Pope

Underwater.

I'd wear a big ol' helmet around my head.

Octopus, pink, sees me.

Go to space.

Moon rocks.

Put them in my rocket.

Sleep in my sleeping bag in space.

Jump off with my astronaut suit.

I would travel to space, go to work, and blast up to Mars.

Probably, I might work on the Moon, work on Mars, work on Earth.

I can get my rocket ready when I go to space.

I'm gonna build another spaceship.

I wanted to travel to the Moon.

In the Milky Way!

My Big Day At WaySub

by Malachi Pope

I got hired at WaySub.

At WaySub, I made the customers some sandwiches. That's what they wanted.

Some ham, some avocados, spinach, coleslaw, cheese, some tomatoes. They ate it, and they liked it.

I made some ham sandwiches, tomatoes, avocados, spinach, and I had some blue gloves on.

They hired me and paid me a lot of money. Probably got paid like 2 million. I want to be a manager.

To be a manager, you gotta get you a little job, make some money, pay your rent and your water bill. Then, when you get a job, you can get your own house.

I can make the best po' boys.

I've been making the best po' boys at Subway for 3 years.

Cheese, mustard, mayo, avocados. The po' boy costs 2 million dollars. I make the best sandwiches and the best po' boys in the whole world.

And I'm the best coach over basketball in PE. I'm the best basketball coach in the whole world.

by Malachi Pope

I Woke Up As A Turtle

by RJ Baker

I woke up one day.

I was a turtle.

Swimming under water

In the ocean.

Saw a shark.

I saw an alligator get up

Then I swim faster

Feeling scared.

Go faster.

Then I saw a baby shrimp.

Then I say "I'm good. How 'bout you?"

Friends.

See an orange fish, Nemo.

Then me and Nemo swim away.

Helped by big fish.

Shark and alligator left.

Then I said, "Goodbye."

Simba

by RJ Baker

My dog like to bark a lot

He tell people to get out.

Jump in doghouse.

He love to eat dog food.

He love to run away.

He love to fight cats.

He love to be loud.

My dog's name is Simba.

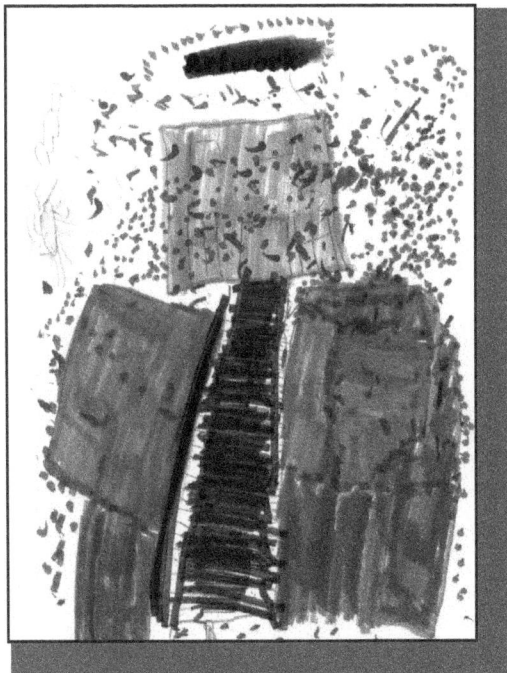

Feeding the Turtles

Black Panther Mystery Case

by Stevanna Knight

If a black panther had a job,

he would be a detective.

Very good at camouflaging.

Go slow and camouflage, like Pink Panther.

He will solve a case.

With a magnifying glass,

find the footprints.

The fox as a witness.

Foxes are pretty sneaky,

but they're sweet too—but sneaky.

Other animals are: the zebra, deer, lion, and monkey.

They find a footprint, but it's hard to tell.

It could be a zebra or a deer.

They go on the cameras.

The security cams are controlled by the sheep.

Dun dun dun dun!

The monkey has been kidnapped!

Along with the gorillas, chimpanzees, and baboons.

The Black Panther and his bunny sidekick figure it out!

They jumped out of the window and saved all the animals.

It was the sheep who was the kidnapper the whole time.

The reason the sheep did it was because

she didn't want the fox to be the president.

She wanted to be the president.

Mystery case solved!

Ninja Turtle, the Problem Solver

by Stevanna Knight

If I were a ninja turtle on their team,

I would wear a dress and a wig (maybe red, black, or brown).

Since I am a turtle and I won't have no hair,

I'm gonna wear some glasses or sunglasses and make myself look good.

On the team, we would not get angry with each other.

I would be the problem solver.

If somebody gets angry with each other,

I would try and make them make up with each other.

But if they don't want help and just wanna keep fighting,

then I will just stop helping you.

Because you're choosing not to want help,

and you're choosing not to need help.

So, my opinion is, if I'm gonna try to help you,

you're gonna have to give me a chance.

Sometimes, I might be the negotiator.

But sometimes, I will be honest—sometimes I don't.

Sometimes people are mean.

Sometimes, just ignore them and try to still be friends
with them.

But if they keep hurting or fighting me for no reason,

I'm not gonna be friends with you.

This is a day in my life as a ninja turtle problem solver.

My Superpower

by Stevanna Knight

The superpower that I would have is absorption.

I want to pick up on other people's powers.

the superpower I have is absorption.

My Underwater Career

by Stevanna Knight

I take pictures. I have a camera. A waterproof camera.
I dive underwater. I take pictures of: blue fish, dolphins,
turtles and octopus. I find seashells. I help pick up crabs and
save dolphins. I use goggles, an air tank and a shovel. This is
my underwater career.

The Turtle's Dream Family

by Shamyah Malone

I met a turtle underwater.

It told me it was happy.

It wanted to eat.

Lettuce and bread.

It wants to form a family.

It had a family that was looking for it, and it was looking for them.

They were swimming in the lake.

They saw him, and they went to each other.

They hugged.

They were happy to see each other.

The turtle had parents and four brothers and four sisters.

They lived happy in the ocean.

Shamyah's Hair Salon Dream

by Shamyah Malone

I'm going to do hair.

Braiding people's hair and getting money.

My business will be called Shamyah's Hair Salon.

If you come in and want braids, it will be $20.

It will be in Gulfport.

I might hire some of my friends.

I'm also going to do nails and toes.

I will have three employees for the hair.

I learned by doing my own hair since I was 12 years old.

We will do your hair when you need it.

The building will be black and white.

My Dream Job

by Vinnie Varnado

My dream job when I grow up is to be the principal of a school.

I will be called "Principal Vinnie."

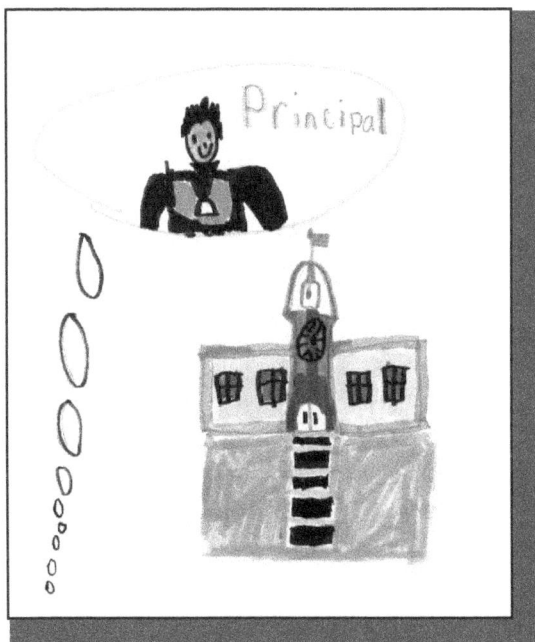

by Vinnie Varnado

Feeding the Turtles

by Vinnie Varnado

I was on the bridge.

I saw ten turtles.

They were pretty good.

They swim slow.

Fed them 30 times.

They act so good.

They jumped to the food.

They took a deep breath.

I saw a gray bird.

It was an eagle.

I saw a big tree.

Feeding the turtles makes me feel happy.

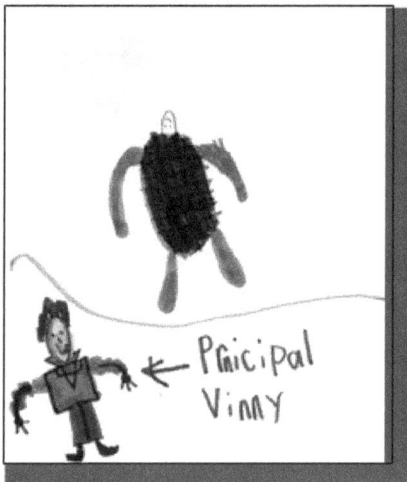

← Principal Vinny

The Magical Turtle Shell

by Zackary Williams

Gives me a wish

A golden credit card with unlimited money

Lots of cars and motorcycles

An automated car - press a button, pick your style/

clothes and it puts on you the clothes that you pick

Have wife and kids

7 room house:

My room, a game room, kids room, library, snake room,

iguana room, guest room

A gray Great Dane

A yacht

Travel to Egypt

A Day In The Life Of A YouTuber/Gamer

by Zackary Williams

YouTube channel

Start recording videos

Games, Minecraft

Record my games so people can learn how to be a pro

Show people how to make buildings, do traps

Show hands-on what to do, the steps, and how to play the game

Get subscribers

Buy a house

Set up a gaming system

All my friends and family can join too

Easy part: talking to people

Most fun part: playing the games

Most challenging part: Editing videos

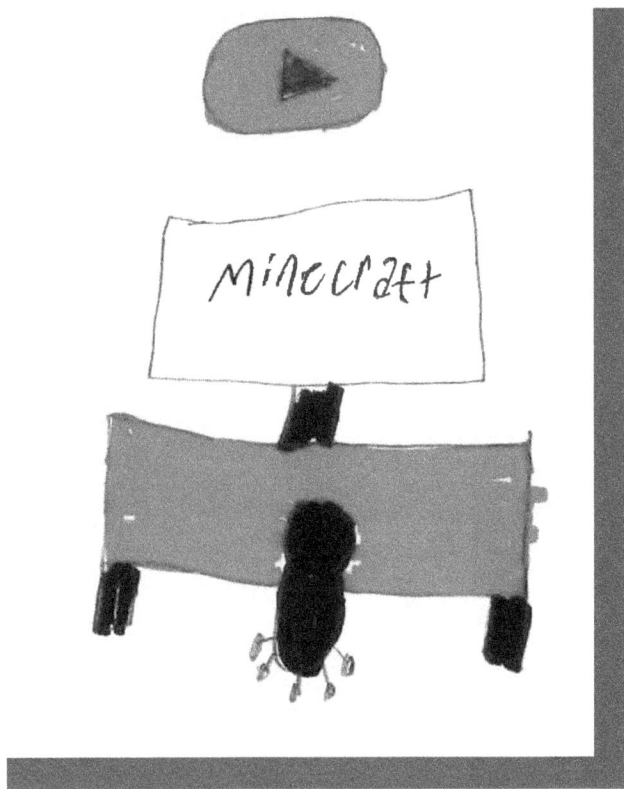

by Zackary Williams

About the Authors

Brionna Mclaurin
Brionna is a junior at West Harrison High School. She enjoys doing nails and hair and having fun with people. Brionna aspires to work in a beauty salon as a hair stylist and nail technician. Her hobbies include playing with her niece and playing outside. Her favorite animal is a Chihuahua.

Courtlan Belcher
Courtlan is a graduate of West Harrison High School. He enjoys playing video games and watching movies. When he grows up, he wants to be a policeman.

Dawson Peoples
Dawson is a graduate of West Harrison High School. He likes dancing and playing basketball. Dawson wants to be a driver and join the Army when he grows up. He enjoys summer, spring break, and Christmas. Dawson has two small dogs.

Donavon Jones
Donavon is a sophomore at West Harrison High School. Donovan's favorite things to do are going out to eat and listening to music. He wants to be a paramedic when he grows up. Donovan likes dogs and rabbits. His favorite color is green and he would like to one day be a captain of a boat.

FaBien McKenzie
FaBien is a graduate of West Harrison High School. Fabien enjoys playing video games and staying indoors. His dream is to become a police officer. His favorite hobby is playing Minecraft.

Jackson Dye
Jackson is a sophomore at West Harrison High School. Jackson likes going fishing, playing video games, and cooking. He wants to be a YouTuber when he grows up. Jackson's favorite animal is the lemur.

Jada Lawrence
Jada is a junior at West Harrison High School. She likes making jewelry, sewing, and coloring. Jada wants to be a hairstylist and nail technician when she grows up. Her favorite animal is dogs.

Juan Serrano-Garcia
Juan is a senior at West Harrison High School. He likes basketball, dancing, and sleeping. His favorite color is red. When he grows up, he wants to be an entertainer.

Kennedi Flowers
Kennedi is a sophomore at West Harrison High School. She enjoys drawing, coloring, watching TikTok, and listening to country music. Kennedi wants to work at Raising Cane's as a cook when she grows up. Her favorite color is pink and her favorite animals are her dogs, Hardy and Bear.

LaDevion Leggett
LaDevion is a graduate of West Harrison High School. He likes to paint and listen to music. He

enjoys browsing pictures of vans and hotels. When he grows up, he wants to be an actor.

Makayla Harris
Makayla is a sophomore at West Harrison High School. She enjoys going fishing, riding her four-wheeler, and playing games. She is part of a big family and has a pond at her house. Makayla wants to be a vet, paramedic, or nail technician when she grows up. Her favorite animals are her dogs, Minnie, Rocky, and Ghost.

Malachi Pope
Malachi is a graduate of West Harrison High School. He likes watching TV and going to the beach. When he grows up, he wants to be a firefighter. Malachi enjoys playing the Wii, and his favorite animal is a monkey.

RJ Baker
RJ is a sophomore at West Harrison High School. He likes playing games and going fishing. When he grows up, he wants to be a police officer. RJ enjoys playing football, and his favorite animal is his pet, Simba.

Shamyah Malone
Shamyah is in 10th grade at West Harrison High School. She enjoys styling hair, playing outdoors, and swimming. Her aspiration is to become a business owner when she grows up.

Stevanna Knight
Stevanna is a senior at West Harrison High School. She likes taking care of her child, crocheting, drawing, doing cross-stitch, playing the guitar,

and playing the violin. Stevanna's favorite animals are cats and dogs. She is currently undecided about her future career.

Vincent Varnado
Vincent is a junior at West Harrison High School. He likes eating Nutty Buddy bars. When he grows up, he wants to be a school principal. Vincent enjoys watching YouTube, Hulu, and playing PS4. His cat's name is Tora.

Zackary Williams
Zackary is a sophomore at West Harrison High School. He likes playing games and Lego building. Zackary has dogs named Stewie, Bella, Athena, and Aphrodite. He wants to be a YouTuber when he grows up with the name "Nightmare."

www.ingramcontent.com/pod-product-compliance
Lightning Source LLC
Chambersburg PA
CBHW051242020426
42331CB00017B/3486